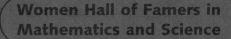

Mae Jemison

The First African American
Woman in Space

Mae Jemison

The First African American
Woman in Space

Magdalena Alagna

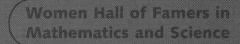
the rosen publishing group's
rosen
central

Published in 2004 by The Rosen Publishing Group, Inc.
29 East 21st Street, New York, NY 10010

Library of Congress Cataloging-in-Publication Data

Alagna, Magdalena.
Mae Jemison : the first African American woman in space /
by Magdalena Alagna. — 1st ed.
    p. cm. — (Women hall of famers in mathematics and science)
Summary: Provides insights into the life of Mae Jemison, the
first female African American astronaut, including some of
the steps she took to reach her goals.
Includes bibliographical references and index.
ISBN 0-8239-3878-6 (lib. bdg.)
    1. Jemison, Mae, 1956–   —Juvenile literature. 2. African
American women astronauts—Biography—Juvenile literature.
3. Astronauts—United States—Biography—Juvenile literature.
[1. Jemison, Mae, 1956– . 2. Astronauts. 3. African
Americans—Biography. 4. Women—Biography.]   I. Title.
II. Series.
TL789.85.J46A43 2003
629.45′0092—dc21
[B]

                                                    2002011132

Manufactured in the United States of America

Contents

Introduction

It was clear from a young age that Mae Jemison would go on to do great things. She first became interested in science when she was only four years old. Throughout her childhood, she pursued interests in anthropology, archaeology, and astronomy—subjects that fascinated and delighted young Mae. She skipped the seventh grade and graduated from high school when she was only sixteen years old. Mae entered Stanford University in California at sixteen, where she was granted a National Achievement Scholarship.

Since her childhood, Mae has achieved a wide variety of impressive goals. She has always used her knowledge to help others. Her undergraduate degrees were put to good use after college. Mae's interest in science helped her with her studies at Cornell medical school. Her interest in African American studies took her to Kenya, where she did an internship during a summer break from medical school. After her studies at Cornell, Mae worked with the Peace Corps in Sierra Leone and Liberia, in West Africa. There, she managed health care for Peace Corps and United States Embassy personnel and worked with the National Institutes of Health (NIH) and the Centers for Disease Control and Prevention (CDC) on several research projects, including development of a hepatitis B vaccine. Mae has devoted much of her time to working with children. One of her projects is a science camp for teens. Other projects have to do with making science and technology classes easier to understand in school systems.

But Mae is best known as the first African American woman in space. She was one of only fifteen people accepted as part of the *Endeavour* space mission. Mae expressed pride in her own heritage on that mission by taking into space a poster of dancer-choreographer Judith Jamison performing "Cry," a dance dedicated to the lives of African American women.

In her lifetime, Mae Jemison has accomplished incredible feats. Not only was she the first black woman to become an astronaut, she also became a doctor, a scientist, and a teacher. Along the way, she made time to learn Japanese, Swahili, and Russian fluently. She serves on the board of directors for several corporations and dedicates herself to helping others by organizing a camp each summer called The Earth We Share (TEWS). How has Mae been able to accomplish so much?

The answer is as straightforward as the woman herself: Mae Jemison has never given in to self-doubt. She says she has had to be "arrogant" in believing steadfastly in her own abilities, even at a young age. Mae was only five years old when a teacher asked her what she wanted to be when she grew up. The young Mae promptly replied that she wanted to be a scientist, to the astonishment of her teacher. Mae accomplished her childhood goal, without stopping to dwell on the obstacles that blocked her path. In the interviews and lectures she gives and even in her autobiography, *Find Where the Wind Goes: Moments from My Life*, Mae's message is more about staying true to yourself and your goals than about dwelling on setbacks or negativity.

1

A Scientist in the Making

Mae Carol Jemison was born in Decatur, Alabama, at Decatur General Hospital on October 17, 1956. She was the youngest of three children. Her father, Charlie, was a maintenance supervisor. Her mother, Dorothy, became a teacher. Mae has an older sister, Ada Sue, and an older brother, Charles, whose nickname is Ricky. In her autobiography, *Find Where the Wind Goes*, Mae claimed that the nurses at the hospital called her Rosebud because of the shape of her lips, and that her father called her Fattening Bug because she grew so quickly as a toddler.

Though she essentially grew up in Chicago, Illinois, away from Decatur

Mae was born in Decatur, Alabama, but was raised in Chicago, Illinois. Chicago provided more opportunities for the Jemison family. Chicago is a bustling city, unlike Decatur, which is a small town. Mae's mother was able to find work easier in Chicago.

where she was born, Mae would revisit Alabama on occasion. Decatur is near Huntsville, Alabama, home of the Marshall Space Flight Center, and Mae would eventually spend much time there during her astronaut training.

According to *Find Where the Wind Goes*, Mae has fond memories of Decatur. Among these memories is a shocking story of how she, as a two-year-old, drove her father's car. As the story goes,

Dorothy and Charlie Jemison and some of their friends had gone shopping with little Mae. They pulled into the parking lot of a store, and Dorothy got out to pick up some groceries. She needed help carrying the bags, so Charlie got out of the car to help her. Mae, right under the noses of Charlie's two friends, clambered into the front seat of Charlie's Buick and managed to pop the clutch, put the car in gear, and hit the gas pedal. However, she was too little to see over the steering wheel, and the car quickly smashed into three parked cars.

HELLO, CHICAGO

When Mae was three years old, the family moved to Chicago. In *Find Where the Wind Goes*, Mae wrote that her mother decided to move to Chicago because there weren't as many opportunities for work in Decatur, Alabama. In fact, Mae recalled visiting Decatur as an adult, and she admitted that it was a sleepy little town. In Decatur at that time, most black women could find work only as maids for white people. Dorothy Jemison had gone to college for two years at Talladega College in Alabama, and she wanted to complete her bachelor's degree. She packed up her three children and moved to Chicago. Charlie Jemison, who had not at first wanted to leave Alabama, followed a few months later. Dorothy did in fact finish her degree and became a schoolteacher. She also went on to get her master's degree. Mae's mom served as a good role model for the young girl. Mae learned early on that a good education was very important.

At first, the Jemisons lived in the Woodlawn section of Chicago. Mae Jemison remembers being afraid of the dark and that her brother and sister would lock her in the basement of their house, with all the lights turned out. Mae Jemison was a self-described "scaredy-cat" who was not only afraid of the dark but also afraid of heights. As a girl, Mae wanted to take dance lessons, but to get to the dance studio she would have to take the "El." The "El" is the elevated train in Chicago that rides above the ground, unlike the subway trains in other cities. Mae didn't dare look down while she was waiting on the train platform. She said that she outgrew her fear of heights when her natural curiosity and love of dancing got the better of her fear. In the face of her overwhelming need to know, all fear was forgotten.

When Mae Jemison was five years old, she had an experience in kindergarten at Woodlawn Elementary School that illustrates a lot about her personality, her drive to succeed, and her confidence in herself. Mae's teacher asked the students what they wanted to be when they grew up. Many of the students said things like police officer, mail carrier, or firefighter. When the teacher called on Mae Mae, she answered loud and clear, "I want to be a scientist." The teacher looked a little confused. It was 1961, and there were not that many opportunities in science for women, not to mention black women. "Don't you mean a nurse?" the teacher asked. "No, I mean a scientist," she said again, making sure that there could be no misunderstanding.

Mae's childhood was spent in Chicago, Illinois. Years after attending school, Mae (second from bottom right) *went to Dumas Elementary School to speak to the students. She spoke of her memories of being in school and surely inspired the students to reach for their goals.*

When Mae's older brother, Ricky, was threatened by a gang member in front of the Jemison house, Dorothy Jemison insisted that the family move out of Woodlawn and into Morgan Park. There was a lot of gang activity in Woodlawn, but there was not as much in Morgan Park. Mae was ten years old when the family moved into Morgan Park, where her family was the first black family on the block. Her teacher from her last school had requested that Mae be allowed to skip the seventh grade and go right into eighth grade because she was able to do eighth-grade work.

EARLY SCIENCE PROJECTS AND STUDY

One of the first science experiments Mae Jemison did was called Eras of Time. It was a study of the evolution of the universe. Mae worked on the project from third until sixth grade. Each year, she spent time after school and during the summers at the library, where she would research different eras of time, such as the Mesozoic era, the time when the dinosaurs lived. She constructed dioramas of each era of time. In the fifth and sixth grades, she came across the work of Doctors Harold Urey and Stanley L. Miller, scientists who worked to understand how life formed on Earth. Urey and Miller's research sparked the girl's curiosity and imagination. Mae loved piecing together the clues of human evolution using information provided in the research

Mae spent a lot of time at the Adler Planetarium during her childhood. The Adler Planetarium opened in Chicago in 1930. It contains artifacts from the history of astronomy, as well as a planetarium theater and a sophisticated observatory.

of prominent scientists such as Urey and Miller. Mae also read many books about dinosaurs.

Everyone in the Jemison family had a library card, and visits to the library were a big part of Mae Jemison's childhood. Dorothy and Charlie Jemison encouraged all of their children to learn. It was during this time that Mae also became fascinated with astronomy, the study of things outside our atmosphere. She often went

Professor and science fiction author Fred Hoyle influenced Mae greatly as a child. Her love of astronomy brought her into the world of science fiction books, which Mae grew to love. In addition to Fred Hoyle's books, Mae also liked Isaac Asimov, Arthur C. Clarke, and Madeleine L'Engle.

to Chicago's Adler Planetarium. It was her love of astronomy that brought her to read Fred Hoyle's books.

Fred Hoyle was a British astronomer. He also wrote science fiction novels, such as *A for Andromeda*. After Mae read this novel, she couldn't get enough of reading science fiction books. She also liked the authors Isaac Asimov and Arthur C. Clarke, as well as Madeleine L'Engle's *Wrinkle in Time* and *The Arm of the Starfish*. She especially liked Madeleine L'Engle's books because they had women scientists as the heroines of the books. However, in her autobiography, Mae wrote that she also identified with the white male heroes of Asimov's and Clarke's books. Mystery and adventure were what allowed her to identify with these characters. In science fiction books, the characters are often going on mysterious adventures. Mae also felt that life was a mysterious adventure.

POLITICS AND SOCIAL SCIENCE

Dorothy and Charlie Jemison always talked about politics and social science with their children, as did their uncle Louis, Charlie's brother. The Jemison children were interested in black history and in figures such as Paul Robeson, an athlete, singer, actor, and activist. At a time when African Americans were still encountering a lot of racial prejudice that kept them from pursuing meaningful careers, Paul Robeson was successful in his chosen career. He was an all-American football player for Rutgers University, and he went on to appear in plays such as *Othello* and also in several films, such as *Showboat*. The family was also influenced by South African singer Miriam Makeba.

As a child, Mae loved Paul Robeson. Here, he stars in Show Boat, *a musical that was released in 1936. In addition to acting, Robeson was a professional football player, the first black player on the Rutgers University football team.*

After seeing her in concert, Dorothy was struck by the singer's natural hairstyle. In the 1960s, many black women were using chemicals to straighten their hair so that it could be styled much the way a white person's hair is styled. However, Makeba wore her hair short and naturally curly. Dorothy decided that she and her girls would wear their hair the same way. For Mae Jemison, this was a good introduction to the civil rights movement that was starting to take hold in the 1960s. The civil rights movement in America was spearheaded by groups such as the NAACP (National Association for the Advancement of Colored People) and by Martin Luther King Jr. in the 1950s and 1960s. The movement raised national awareness in America about the way blacks were treated, and it resulted in the Civil Rights Act of 1964, which made discrimination against people based on their color, race, or religion against the law. Malcolm X and Stokely Carmichael, two important figures in the civil rights movement, were often discussed in the Jemison household. Malcolm X was a militant black leader who was assassinated in 1965. Stokely Carmichael, a prominent figure in the civil rights movement, chanted the phrase "Black Is Beautiful" at a student rally in 1965.

There were riots across the United States during the summers of the mid-1960s. In the summer of 1968, Mae Jemison was twelve years old. It was the year that Martin Luther King Jr., an important leader in the civil rights movement,

Mae grew up with an awareness of the civil rights movement. Her mother made sure that the Jemison children knew about civil rights leaders such as Malcolm X and Martin Luther King Jr., pictured here during the March on Washington where he delivered his famous "I Have a Dream" speech.

was shot, and Mae Jemison remembers cowering in her house in Chicago to escape a riot that was going on just blocks from her house. Running to the front window, she peeped outside and saw crowds of people on the street, among which were the National Guard. Mae was scared, even though some of the National Guardsmen were black. Children had been killed during the riots, and Mae did not trust that the soldiers would protect her. Then she reminded herself that she was just as much a part of the United States as the soldiers were. It was a scary but ultimately empowering experience for the young girl. She never forgot that everyone must contribute to making the world a better place and that each person must do his or her part for peace, knowledge, and understanding.

HIGH SCHOOL PLAYS AND PROJECTS

Mae Jemison entered high school when she was just twelve years old. She was tall for her age, already about five feet six inches of what would eventually be her full height of five feet nine inches. She was not totally intimidated by all the older kids because of her height and also because she wanted to study so badly. In high school, she had the opportunity to study physics, chemistry, and biology. She also continued to love dancing, and she tried out for cheerleading and school plays. There was so much to do in high school that she didn't have much time to be intimidated because she was one of the youngest first-year students. During her senior year, she was even the student council president.

Mae studied Russian throughout her four years of high school. She was convinced that Russian would be an important language to know when she was working in the scientific community. Surprisingly, Mae got a D in gym class during her first semester in high school. Mae had a hard time keeping her gym shoes polished brightly enough to satisfy her gym teacher. This D in gym was a good lesson in humility for the confident young girl. Another lesson was trying out for the school production of *West Side Story*. Although Mae was a good dancer, she couldn't sing a note. She decided to try out anyway, and when the director heard her sing, she had to kiss the star part she wanted good-bye. Instead, Mae was given a part in the chorus.

When she was fifteen, Mae worked at Cook County Hospital, in the hematology lab. (Hematology is the study of the blood.) Mae was hired to do research for a project about sickle-cell anemia, a deadly disease that mainly affects African Americans. It was during this project that Mae began to understand that she not only had to run experiments and collect data. If she wanted to be a scientist, she would have to come up with hypotheses to test. This was a big step for the young girl who initially hadn't even wanted to call the hematology lab to ask whether she would be allowed to work on her project there. She under-stood what learning experiences she could have if she just persevered in spite of her initial fear.

With all of her science projects and student council work, it would seem that Mae didn't have much time for fun. But high school was not all work and no play. Mae spent time with friends and even dated a little, although she was not technically allowed to go out on dates until she was sixteen. She also had time to engage in a few good pranks with her brother and sister. Once she dumped a bucket of ice water on her brother when he was asleep!

At sixteen years old, Mae Jemison was ready for her next adventure. She would be going to college at Stanford University in California.

Off to College

2

Mae Jemison was sixteen years old when she started college at Stanford University in California. She had received a National Achievement Scholarship, given by the National Merit Scholarship Program in Evanston, Illinois. The scholarship had been sponsored by Bell Labs. Mae had never been to California, and she was both excited and a little scared as she boarded the plane with a suitcase full of clothes that she had made herself. There were a few reasons why she chose Stanford University. Stanford had famous scientists such as Dr. Linus Pauling on the faculty. Pauling was the only person in the world to have won two unshared Nobel Prizes, one in

1954 for chemistry and one in 1962 for peace, for trying to stop the atmospheric testing of nuclear weapons. Stanford had radio telescopes on campus, great engineering and medical programs, and the Stanford Linear Accelerator Center (SLAC). The SLAC is a national laboratory operated by Stanford University for the U.S. Department of Energy. It is a famous research center that does important and high-profile work.

Stanford also had a great football team. Mae was (and still is) a self-described football fanatic. At Stanford she would not only watch football, she would play on the coed intramural football leagues. Stanford also was a place for great political activism and social awareness. Stanford University was known as the Farm. It was the first school to have coeducational dormitories with girls and boys living on the same floor. That was a big deal at the time, and magazine articles were written about it.

EXPERIENCING RACISM

Mae got scholarship offers from all of the schools to which she applied, including the Massachusetts

Many things about Stanford University appealed to Mae Jemison when she was deciding where to attend college. One important factor in her decision was that Linus Pauling (pictured here), *the two-time Nobel Prize winner, taught at the school.*

Institute of Technology, Cornell University, and Rensselaer Polytechnic Institute. When she got to Stanford, she was confident that she was prepared for biomedical engineering. Biomedical engineering is a scientific discipline in which the principals of mathematics, science, and medicine are applied to the study of technology. However, it wasn't clear to her whether biomedical engineering at Stanford University was ready for her. When she met her adviser during a student orientation event held at his house, Mae was struck by the fact that she was not only one of the few women there, she was the only black person there. People seemed to be friendly to each other, but they didn't talk to her much, not even when she tried to join in the conversation. She had gone to an integrated high school where there were students of many different races and ethnic backgrounds. She had been the student council president, and she was not used to being overlooked either academically or socially. At Stanford, it appeared that she would be judged by her appearance, her gender, and the color of her skin. Although she had sometimes disagreed with teachers in high school, they had never doubted that she was capable of doing well academically. It would take her a while to find her way at Stanford.

During her first semester, she took calculus, solid analytic geometry, introductory chemistry, a freshman seminar on women's physiology, a freshman English class focused on African American literature, and tennis. She was especially excited about chemistry because it had been one of her favorite subjects in high school. However, her professor turned out to be every bit as difficult as she had been warned that he was. Mae sat in the front row of the lecture hall and participated in class, asking questions. She was excited because she was learning about things that interested her. But the professor would either ignore her questions or make her feel stupid for having asked them. When a white male asked the same questions, however, the teacher would praise him for his insight. Mae finally took the not-so-subtle hint and stopped asking questions.

CHANGING TRACKS

Mae got a new adviser, whose specialty was biomedical engineering, during the second quarter of her freshman year. Mae first had become aware of biomedical engineering as a profession during a two-week program that she attended during the summer before her senior year in high school.

Scientists at the University of Illinois showed the students how to perform lab experiments in biomedical engineering. Biomedical engineers are scientists that develop artificial organs and limbs. They also deal with tissue regeneration and develop bionic body parts like computer-operated hands for people who've lost their hands in accidents. One example of a device developed by biomedical engineers is the pacemaker. It is a machine that is implanted in a person's chest to regulate the rhythm of his or her heart. Mae was attracted to biomedical engineering because she loved science and was good at many different branches of it. This was a field that required a knowledge of many different scientific fields, including chemistry, biology, and physics.

But Mae's new adviser believed she should get a degree in chemical engineering, instead of biomedical engineering. Chemical engineering is a science that applies the principles of chemistry, the study of substances, to engineering, which is the designing and making of products that are useful to people. He advised her to do that because biomedical engineering was a new field at that time, and its course of study was not fixed—it was sort of like designing your own major. If she took chemical engineering, everyone would know that she had gone through a rigorous program and had gotten a classical science degree. Not only that, but chemical engineering required most, if not all, of the same courses that a degree in biomedical engineering would have, plus a few more.

Because the Jemisons had always encouraged their children to be well-rounded, Jemison wanted to take some language courses at Stanford. She had taken four years of Russian in high school and was convinced that speaking Russian was an important qualification for a scientist to have. Why didn't she take Russian at Stanford? She had asked her first adviser how to figure out which courses she should take in the Russian language, and he had answered, "If they have not contacted you, just assume you should take beginning Russian." Mae was embarrassed that she might

At Stanford University, Mae experienced many challenges. Not only was she younger than most of the students, she was also one of only a few black women studying science. She overcame these challenges, however, and also went on to lead the Black Student Union.

not have done well enough on her placement exams to take a more advanced Russian course, even after studying it for four years in high school. She was so embarrassed that she did not even go to the Russian studies department to inquire what her score was. She took Swahili instead, partly because she thought she would like it, and partly because her older sister Ada Sue had taken Swahili in college. This was not the only African course that she took during her first year. She also took African dance courses.

Although she would later live in Roble Hall, where many African American students lived, she did not start out rooming there. She was at the Alondra House, and was the youngest person in the dorm. This at times led to funny situations, such as when Mae got a traffic ticket and had to take someone in the dorm, someone older than eighteen years of age, with her to traffic court. Mae made friends in her dorm that were to last a lifetime. One friend from Alondra House, Linda Jones, years later became an anchor on the Houston, Texas, evening news, and she covered Mae's launch into space.

AFRICAN AND AFRICAN AMERICAN STUDIES

During her sophomore year, Mae took a political science class called Politics in Sub-Saharan Africa. She also became the president of the Black Student Union, an organization that represented the black students on campus. This representation included providing a place where black students could voice their concerns and where they could be sure of gaining help to address those concerns. The Black Student Union also was a social organization where people could make friends. Mae designed and helped to teach a class called Race and Politics in Education and one called Race and Culture in the Caribbean. She continued to take classes in Swahili and African history, culture, and politics. During the fall of her senior year, she found she needed just two required courses to get a bachelor of arts degree in African and Afro-American studies. Chemical engineering had the most required courses of any field of study at Stanford. Mae was also juggling extracurricular activities and a social life. How and why did she find time to complete all of the requirements for a bachelor of arts degree in African studies?

Mae recalled in her autobiography that the professors in the African studies department welcomed her into their classes and wanted her there.

Their attitude was a welcome change from that of many of her chemical engineering professors, who did not give her any indication that they believed in her ability to do the work. Mae believes that she was unconsciously balancing the poor reception that she got in the science curriculum with the positive reception she got in the social sciences.

ROLE MODELS

Mae graduated from Stanford University with a bachelor of science degree in chemical engineering and qualified for a bachelor of arts degree in African and Afro-American studies. Throughout her college experience, Mae had some role models who helped her to remember all that she was striving to accomplish. These role models were people who were making a difference in the world. For instance, Gloria Steinem, a now-famous feminist, was at that time a journalist who brought to the public's attention how women were thought of in our culture and what need there was for feminism and radical change in people's attitudes toward

Gloria Steinem, shown here in 1972, influenced Mae Jemison's feminist beliefs. Mae was often faced with discrimination because of her race and gender. Strong female role models inspired Mae to persevere and to try to make a difference in the world.

women. Mae studied Julius Nyerere, the president of Tanzania, a country in East Africa. She was fascinated with how Nyerere worked to keep Tanzania free of the politics of both the Soviet Union and the United States. It was not an easy thing for a small country to avoid the influences of two such powerful countries, and Mae saw in Nyerere's leadership a way to navigate her own life, taking from the strong what she needed to survive, but without compromising herself.

However inspirational these people were for Mae, she cites as her real role models the people she knew growing up—the members of her family and her teachers. It was from them that she learned the importance of knowledge, of applying knowledge, of being well-rounded and self-reliant. Her uncle Louis was the one who had introduced her to Albert Einstein's theory of relativity. Her aunt Melvyn, who worked at a dry cleaner's, took Mae to work with her and taught her about the importance of working hard and doing a job well and with pride. Her brother and sister taught her how to play chess. Her father taught her how to play a game called bid whist, which is similar to the card game bridge.

Stanford University had been an eye-opening experience for the smart, ambitious young woman. However, she wrote in her autobiography that she did not really learn how to study until she reached medical school. It was there that she would discover that, no matter how smart you were, there was no escaping studying every day, after having been in class from nine to five!

3

Becoming Doctor Jemison

Mae Jemison spent the summer after she graduated college working as an engineer at IBM in San Jose, California. Then, at twenty years old, she went to Cornell University Medical College (CUMC) in New York City. She specifically wanted to be in New York City for medical school, and Cornell is one of the best medical schools in the United States. She brought with her to Cornell a solid scientific background, but she did not really consider herself a premed student. She did not intend to practice medicine. She was taking a degree in medicine to pursue her goal of working in biomedical engineering. It was applying scientific and medical technology to help people and better their quality of life that really attracted Mae to medical school. Therefore, when she met her new roommate and saw her sprawled over a desk spread with textbooks, Mae was confused. Classes didn't start for two days. She hadn't even gotten her textbooks yet, and here, her roommate had already begun studying!

Luckily for Mae, the students got together to play bid whist to get to know each other before classes started. This was the card game that her father had taught her how to play. Mae showed her feminist streak by helping the women's bid whist team to win when they competed against the men.

Medical school did not have a big, organized orientation session like they had at college. The students got their schedules and the information about the physical exams and vaccinations that they needed. But none of this prepared Mae for gross anatomy class. It was in this class that students learned about muscles, internal organs, blood vessels, bones, and nerves. They learned all this by dissecting a human body. A dissecting manual was one of the books that Mae's roommate had been studying just days before. Mae, however, had never done anything that could have prepared her to dissect a human cadaver. There wasn't even a lecture first. The students put on their lab coats and went into the lab to dissect. It was during this time that Mae realized she had better start studying hard. She was almost totally lost during that first gross anatomy class. She was, however, proud of herself for conquering her fear and actually touching an exposed muscle.

It took her about two weeks to learn the medical vocabulary she needed to feel comfortable dissecting cadavers in gross anatomy lab. As for her other classes, at first Mae thought that her roommate and friends were being too picky by concentrating on memorizing details such as the names of minor blood vessels. They made a game out of it, giving each other pop quizzes and challenging each other to know the right answers. Sometimes they even sneaked into the gross anatomy lab at night to

Mae studied hard at Cornell Medical School, located in New York City. For the first time in her life, she had to become fully immersed in her studies just to be able to get by in her classes. One of these classes required her to dissect a human cadaver. This experience prepared her for tough challenges that lay ahead.

go over what they had done that day and to imprint it in their memories. Mae didn't do anything of the kind. She thought that it would be enough for the students to understand the mechanics of the body and how everything works. One day she asked her teacher during a lecture on an artery abnormality if they were expected to remember even the smallest details. After staring at her hard for a moment, he explained that she would, in fact, need to pay attention to such details.

Although she had studied in the afternoons at Stanford, she had never been used to pulling all-nighters, doing so only twice in her undergraduate career. When she got to medical school, it was a common practice for her to study until two o'clock in the morning. In her autobiography, Mae recounted the experience of being so caught up in her class work that she would meet new people and imagine seeing their body parts. She imagined what it would be like if a person she was talking to was accidentally hit with a spear during the conversation. Which structures of the body would she be able to see? Which would be damaged, depending on the angle that the spear hit? These were the same as many of the questions asked in gross anatomy exams.

FUN, POLITICS, AND SOCIAL ACTIVISM

Mae continued to take African dance classes. In New York, she studied with Katherine Dunham, a well-known dancer who was renowned for her techniques. Mae's roommate, Joan, also taught her how to play pool. The young women also played basketball games in the gym at school. Many of the premed students played basketball to relax and blow off some steam. The games were coed, and they could sometimes get aggressive.

Of course, Mae enjoyed many of the delights of being in New York City. New York is home to the Alvin Ailey dance troupe, a troupe of dancers that Mae greatly admired. Not only did she take some classes at the Alvin Ailey dance studio, she went to see the troupe perform, as well as seeing the New York City Ballet and plays.

Drawing on her talent for performance, which she had not done since high school, Mae wrote a funny sketch with her roommate, Joan. They and their friend Blaine performed the skit for the class Christmas show. It was a skit about one of their stuffy professors becoming lost in Harlem and being propositioned by a woman on a street corner. The woman was Mae herself, dressed in hot pants and high-heeled boots.

Some of the extracurricular activities that Mae was involved in were purely for fun. Some happened to be fun but were also for the betterment of others. For instance, during her first year in medical school, Mae helped to put together a publication for high school students about the dangers of prescription drug abuse. She did this with a friend, Rupa Redding. They went into the area high schools to distribute the publication and to talk to the students about prescription drug abuse. During her second year, she helped to put together a health and law fair with students at Columbia University Law School, and with medical students from New Jersey Medical and Dental, New York University, Cornell, and Columbia. At the time, she was the president of the Cornell chapter of the Student National Medical Association. During her third year, Mae was elected president of the Cornell Student Executive Committee, and during her final year in medical school, she was Cornell's student representative to the Association of American Medical Colleges.

During a summer break from medical school, Mae traveled to Kenya, Africa (Nairobi, the capital of Kenya, is pictured here), *to work with a group of doctors called the Flying Doctors. Together they traveled to small towns and provided medical care to those that needed it. Helping people has always been a priority of Mae's.*

If dissection labs were a challenge in Mae's first year in medical school, there was a surprise waiting for her during her second year, in the form of microbiology lab. In this lab, students would experiment with blood to understand how antibodies are produced as a result of vaccinations, such as the typhoid vaccination. There was just one little thing on which Mae hadn't counted—the students would be supplying the blood for the experiments. Mae recalled in her autobiography that her lab partner had a difficult time getting the blood from her arm and that, in fact, the professor had to do it. But also during her second year, Mae took a class called physical diagnosis and was granted her medical instruments. The class taught students how to do the things doctors do during physical checkups, such as take blood pressure, listen to heartbeat and breathing, check reflexes, and examine the eyes and ears. "Owning a stethoscope meant you really were becoming a doctor," she wrote in her autobiography. The instruments were expensive, so she skimped where she could. For instance, she didn't order the classic black doctor bag and used a cheaper bag instead. The only thing that was difficult for Mae was learning how to ask people to take off their clothes so that she could examine them naked. She managed to make it comfortable for the patient, but she remained embarrassed!

INTERNSHIP IN KENYA, AFRICA

In the summer between her second and third years of medical school, Mae went to Kenya, a country in Africa. Going to Kenya seemed to bring together many of Mae's interests, such as African culture, medicine, and helping others. She went to Kenya on a grant from the International Travelers Association. Although she had fun going to game parks, places where people can see wild animals in their natural habitat, Mae also worked hard. She hooked up with the Flying Doctors, a part of the African Medical and Research Foundation (AMREF). This group of doctors and other Western health care professionals went into little-traveled areas of East Africa to provide medical care and health services, even including surgery, to people who had none of those services or care. Mae did community health service work for this group, walking door to door in villages and measuring the health of the people, recording the height and weight of the children, and seeing how many of these people were vaccinated for certain dis-eases. She also assisted with surgery and worked in a hospital and clinic.

As always with Mae, she managed to have a lot of fun while working hard. Nairobi, the capital city of Kenya, had movie theaters, and Mae managed to see *Moonraker*, a James Bond movie, in one of them. She also enjoyed some of the more mundane things women do, such as going to the hair salon. It was a big kick for her to be able to walk into any hair salon and have her hair done right, which didn't always happen in America. Most important, she liked the sense of belonging that she felt being among Africans. After eight weeks of living and working in Kenya, she traveled to Egypt and Israel. She had two weeks to do all of this traveling before she had to get back to her third year of medical school. She went to Egypt and saw the pyramids, Luxor Temple, and the Nile. She even saw King Tut's tomb. In Israel, she stayed on a kibbutz with a woman she'd met on the plane coming into Israel.

When she got back to Cornell, she discovered medical rotations. Students doing rotations stay up for thirty-six hours straight, checking on patients in hospitals. The experience taught her that she could still be effective and think clearly after many hours with no sleep. After finishing medical school, she had a degree in medicine. That did not mean that she could practice medicine; for that, she needed a license. And to get a license, she needed to complete an internship and get a residency. A residency gives new doctors experience in specialized areas of medicine, such as obstetrics or pediatrics. Mae had never intended to practice medicine, so she wasn't sure that she wanted to get into a residency program. In such a program, new doctors get paid very little and work about eighty hours a week, learning the ropes from experienced doctors. She had graduated from medical school. What would she do next?

4

The Peace Corps and Applying to NASA

Mae Jemison had enjoyed her experience in Kenya. For that reason, she seized the opportunity to spend the summer between her third and fourth years of medical school in a refugee camp in Thailand. Refugees are people who flee their country because it is dangerous. They seek a safe place in another, more peaceful, country. Many Cambodians had fled from the war in their country to Thailand. Mae helped them recover from their health problems, such as malnutrition, tuberculosis (a lung ailment), and dysentery (a disease marked by severe diarrhea; the disease is usually caused by bacteria in contaminated water). After she graduated medical school, Mae figured that the best way to ensure that she would get back to pursuing her interest in practicing medicine in developing countries was simple: She would take a one-year internship, with nothing planned after it. She figured that having nothing planned would force her to live up to her dream of working in a developing country, instead of going into a residency program in the United States. Usually, students planned their residencies after their internship, but Mae did not, even though her professors tried to convince her that she was making a mistake. During a residency, young doctors work a lot of hours under the supervision of more experienced doctors to learn a wide variety of specialized branches of medicine. But Mae's objectives were clear to her. She wanted to do some work in developing countries for a while, then go on to do graduate work in engineering, specifically doing biomedical engineering research.

Mae did her internship year in Los Angeles at the Los Angeles County/University of Southern California Medical Center (LAC/USC). She spent

Mae, pictured here after being chosen to work for NASA, explored different careers in her lifetime. She utilized her medical skills and willingness to help others by joining the Peace Corps after medical school. There, she worked very hard. She didn't know it at the time, but she was preparing herself for the rigors of astronaut training.

the year as a general practitioner, which means that she did not specialize in one area of medicine, but treated everyone from babies to the elderly. During this time, she was still looking for ways that she could practice medicine in developing countries. She applied to many organizations, writing that she could work as either a physician or an engineer, whichever they needed her to be. Eventually, the Peace Corps offered her a position in West Africa.

LIVING AND WORKING IN WEST AFRICA

From 1983 to 1985, Mae was with the Peace Corps in West Africa. The Peace Corps is an organization that was started in 1961 by President John F. Kennedy. The organization's mission is to send volunteers to developing countries in Africa, Asia, South America, and anywhere else they are needed. The volunteers help the citizens of those countries in whatever area they need help, such as in health care, agriculture, and education. Sometimes the volunteers help to set up better school systems or health care clinics. Sometimes the volunteers help people learn more efficient ways of growing food.

Mae served as the area Peace Corps medical officer for Sierra Leone and Liberia. That means she was the general manager for the Peace Corps' health care system in those two areas. What does a general manager do? Mae Jemison was only twenty-six years old, and she was responsible for taking care of the health of all the U.S. Peace Corps volunteers, staff members, embassy personnel of

Countries:
Kenya

World Wise Schools

Water in Africa

PEACE CORPS

About the Project   Resources   Lesson Plans   Help   Learning Community

Home

PCV Kim Shumlansky is with Mama Jerry in the tea fields. The altitude and heavy rains of Kangaita are good conditions for the tea to grow.

by John and Kim Shumlansky
Kangaita, Kenya (1999)

Back

The Peace Corps Web site provides an idea of what the organization is all about. It gives a look into the kind of work that volunteers do and has details of the daily lives of volunteers. This section of the Web site explains the Peace Corps Water in Africa program.

Sierra Leone, and the Peace Corps volunteers in Liberia. She managed a medical office, a laboratory, a pharmacy, and volunteer health training. She was also the primary care doctor, which meant that everybody went to her first before being assigned to another doctor. All of the volunteers came to her for their assignments, too. She was on call twenty-four hours a day, seven days a week, for two and a half years.

During her time in West Africa, Mae Jemison treated diseases that she had only read about in textbooks. She worked with some of the best doctors and nurses in Sierra Leone. The medical equipment was, at times, barely adequate for their purposes. It was always a challenge to get the supplies and the equipment needed. While she was working in Sierra Leone, Mae not only helped others as a doctor, she tried to help them take care of their own health. She wrote manuals for self-care. She wrote and enforced guidelines for public health and safety. She did research on a hepatitis B vaccine, rabies, and schistosomiasis, an illness that you can get from any one of five species of waterborne flatworms called schistosomes. The parasite can also be found in snails, which is why the disease is sometimes called snail fever. She did this work with the help of two prestigious health organizations in America, the National Institutes of Health (NIH) and the Centers for Disease Control and Prevention (CDC).

Mae was proud of the work that she did there. According to *Black Explorers* by Catherine

Reef, she said, "I was doing work that affected people's lives and whether they lived or died. I learned to trust myself and work with myself and develop the confidence that I'm able to take care of things on my own."

Mae returned to Los Angeles in the summer of 1985. She spent two years working as a general practitioner—a doctor that does not specialize in any one area of medicine—at CIGNA health plans of California.

THE ROAD TO NASA

Jemison applied to NASA, the National Aeronautics and Space Administration, in 1985. Before NASA officials had a chance to review her application, the space shuttle *Challenger* blew up on January 28, 1986, just seventy-three seconds after liftoff. All seven crew members were killed, including Christa McAuliffe, a high school teacher from New Hampshire, and Ronald McNair, an African American astronaut.

On January 28, 1986, the Challenger *exploded after launching. The accident was a shock to many, and the entire country grieved for those aboard the ship. Here, the* Challenger *smokes and fumes seconds after the accident.*

It was unclear whether there would be a space shuttle program at all after this tragedy. NASA stopped the next fourteen shuttle missions, saying that they would be rescheduled when scientists learned why such an accident had happened. They also wanted to learn how they could prevent something like that from ever happening again. Mae Jemison, although she was as shocked and sad as anyone else was about what had happened to the crew members of the *Challenger*, reapplied to NASA when the space shuttle missions were resumed.

NASA AND THE SPACE RACE

NASA, the National Aeronautics and Space Administration, is the organization that runs the U.S. space program. President Dwight D. Eisenhower started the organization on October 1, 1958. Its main location was on Florida's Merritt Island, a few miles from Cape Canaveral, at what is now called the Kennedy Space Center. In 1961,

Continued on page 62

Continued from page 61

President John F. Kennedy ordered the construction of the Manned Spacecraft Center near Houston, Texas. This would be where the astronauts were trained and space flights were planned. It is also where spacecraft would be developed. It opened in 1963 and would come to be called the Lyndon B. Johnson Space Center (JSC), named for the former president.

At that time, the former Soviet Union was making advances in space exploration, and the United States did not want to be left behind in what would come to be known as the Space Race. The Soviet Union had launched *Sputnik 1*, the first space capsule, in October 1957. A few weeks later, *Sputnik 2* was launched, with a dog named Laika aboard. That was the first space capsule that was launched with a living thing on board the spacecraft. The United States did not launch space capsules until 1958. President Kennedy, who became president in 1961, devoted much time and effort to funding America's space program.

In April 1961, Yuri A. Gagarin was the first human to go into space. He orbited Earth for almost two hours in *Vostok 1*. In February 1962, John Glenn became the first American in space. He orbited Earth three times in *Friendship 7*. The United States did not put a woman in space until 1983, when Sally Ride went up in *Challenger*. Valentina Tereshkova, a cosmonaut, or Soviet astronaut, had gone into space nearly twenty years earlier, in 1963, aboard *Vostok 6*.

Although there had been women in space, and there had been African Americans in space, Mae C. Jemison became the first African American woman to visit space.

Sally Ride, shown here aboard the Challenger *space shuttle in 1983, was the first American woman in space.*

From a very young age, Mae dreamed of being an astro-naut. Here, Mae sits aboard a space shuttle trainer at the Johnson Space Center in Houston, Texas, in August 1987. Although many young people dream of one day going into space, very few actually follow that path. Mae's determination and drive helped her to succeed.

Mae was ecstatic when she got a call asking her if she could come to the Johnson Space Center (JSC) in Houston, Texas, for interviews. Out of the 2,000 people that had applied to the space shuttle program, NASA interviewed about 100 of them, and Mae Jemison was going to be one of them. She desperately wanted to go, but she worried about how to get the time off from her work at CIGNA without anyone knowing where she had gone. All of her life, people had given her mixed signals about her desire to be an astronaut. Her parents were always supportive, but Mae could never tell whether they really believed in her dream or if they were just humoring her. Others were downright negative about her chances for success in the astronaut program. Mae decided to keep this interview a secret until she found out whether she had been chosen or not. She told only the office manager, because she needed to get time off from work. In her autobiography, Mae wrote, "Believe it or not, I was as excited or more so when called for the astronaut interview than when I was selected. Why? Because, I had looked good on paper! My college and medical school transcripts that I fretted over were fine."

THE INTERVIEW

Always one to be prepared, Mae read books about the history of space exploration before she went to her interview at the JSC. Astronaut interviews take one week. Medical exams and checkups are given to make sure that the candidates are perfectly healthy. Being in space is an abnormal environment for the human body to be in. Therefore, NASA wants to make sure that astronauts are in the most healthy condition that they can be in before they get placed into the abnormal, stressful environment of outer space. Astronauts can't have any chronic illnesses, such as diabetes, or any physiologic abnormalities, like heart arrhythmia, a condition that means your heartbeat is irregular. Those interviewing to become astronauts take eye exams to test their eyesight, blood tests, muscle strength tests, hearing tests, and psychological tests. Mae wrote in her autobiography, "A personal favorite was an isolation/claustrophobia test where I was asked to sit inside a three-foot-diameter balloon with air blowing in it for thirty minutes. I was to write my impressions of the experience afterwards as well as write up any modifications I would make to the sphere as a rescue device. I got in and started to hum and sing to myself, then fell asleep. The operator said I was the first one he had seen do that."

However, not everything went perfectly smooth for Mae during her interview. One of her physical checkups showed that she had a heart murmur. Sometimes having a heart murmur means that there is something wrong with your heart, but sometimes a murmur is just a murmur and there is nothing wrong with the heart. Mae explained to the doctor that she knew all about the heart murmur. When she was in medical school, a doctor told her about it. He also told her it was called a functional flow murmur, which meant that there was nothing wrong with her heart. Mae had to get a special heart test called an echocardiogram to see whether her heart was OK. She was relieved to find out that it was fine and that she was still in the running to be an astronaut.

5

NASA and the *Endeavour*

Mae went back to work, where everyone had found out about her trip to NASA, despite all of her attempts at secrecy. Weeks passed, during which some of her friends called to tell Mae that they had been questioned by the FBI about her. This is a routine part of the background check for astronauts. Mae also talked with the FBI. Business continued as usual. Mae worked at CIGNA during the day and took graduate classes in engineering and business at UCLA at night. One day in June 1987, she got the call that she had been selected as an astronaut. She had been one of the fifteen people chosen out of about 2,000 applicants. She was asked not to tell anyone until the next day, when a press release would be broadcast on television news and in newspapers, telling everyone who had been selected to the astronaut program. It was difficult for Mae not to tell anyone; she just had to call her parents and tell them. She also told her cat, Sneeze, whom she had gotten as a little kitten in Sierra Leone. According to her autobiography, "I told Sneeze we were moving to Houston. He was completely cool with it."

ASTRONAUT TRAINING

There is a long process between getting accepted into NASA's astronaut training program and actually becoming an astronaut. There are many different parts of the training, which lasts for about a year but can take longer, depending on the mission for which candidates are being groomed. Astronauts must be physically healthy, but they must also be psychologically and emotionally healthy. NASA also wants well-rounded people

Training at the Johnson Space Center included a lot of unexpected exercises, such as this firefighting exercise. Astronauts are trained to be prepared for anything that might arise. For this reason, NASA makes sure its astronauts are well-rounded and capable of thinking clearly in an emergency.

who can work well with others but who have the strength of personality to be able to make good decisions if they have to. According to *And Not Afraid to Dare*, a book that explores the lives of ten inspirational African American women, "Astronauts are expected to be team players and highly skilled generalists with just the right amount of individuality and self-reliance to be effective crew members."

Astronauts are trained to make sure that they know everything they need to know while they are onboard a spacecraft. The first thing that has to be done with the new members of NASA is to make sure that everyone has the same common starting point of knowledge about space flight. The class of new astronauts in which Mae Jemison found herself came from a variety of different backgrounds, including a meteorologist (a scientist who studies weather), a mechanical engineer, and herself, a medical doctor. The class studied many subjects, such as oceanography, navigation, mathematics, and astronomy.

The class also did some hands-on training outside of the classroom. This included parachute training and survival training on supersonic aircraft. They had to learn this because astronauts use supersonic aircraft in emergency situations. They also did scuba diving and land-and-sea survival training. This is important because astronauts need to be prepared for whatever happens. Of course no one at NASA plans for a spacecraft to make an

Astronauts are trained to excel in a variety of environments and situations. Here, Mae is completing a parachute exercise. Although parachuting is not a part of a regular space mission, it's important that astronauts are taught different methods of survival in case something goes wrong.

The insignia of the STS-47 space flight was designed by the crew members. Each member's name is listed, and an American and Japanese flag are shown side by side to represent the joint mission.

emergency landing in the middle of the ocean, but mistakes can happen. Astronauts learn what to do in any emergency.

The class also learned all about spacecraft and how to be in orbit. They learned about weightlessness, which is what happens when the human body gets into outer space and escapes gravity. Gravity is what holds us down. When there is no gravity, the body experiences weightlessness—it floats. The class learned about the history and dangers of space flight, and what had happened to cause the *Challenger* accident. They learned about every part of a space shuttle, as well as about planets, weather patterns, and geology.

MAE'S ROLE

Mae would be the mission specialist on the space flight. That meant that she was not expected to learn how to fly the supersonic aircraft. She just had to know how to handle the radios, how to fly straight, how to follow headings and flight courses, how to control the aircraft when it was off the ground, and how to plan the flight. She would have many responsibilities. She had to do work to make sure the craft ran well. She might also be taking space walks. But the main task was to oversee and to participate in the many scientific experiments that would be done aboard her ship, the *Endeavour*.

In August 1988, at the end of her training, Mae Jemison became an astronaut. All she had to do was wait for a mission. While the astronauts

On September 20, 1992, the Endeavour *was ready to return to Earth. Here, Mae and Mamoru Mohri prepare for descent. The skills they learned during training were of great help while on the eight-day mission.*

were waiting for a mission, they continued to train. Those who were selected to be on the *Endeavour* trained for two years, much of the time in Japan, to learn about the experiments they would be conducting when the *Endeavour* went into orbit. In Japan, they met and trained with Dr. Mamoru Mohri, who would be on the crew of the *Endeavour*. He was the first Japanese national to fly in a space shuttle.

MEETING LIEUTENANT UHURU

Many exciting things happened to Mae as a result of her being part of NASA. One of them was completely unexpected: She met Nichelle Nichols, the actress who played the character of Lieutenant Uhuru on *Star Trek*. Mae is a huge *Star Trek* fan, and Nichols was doing a *Star Trek* convention in Florida, near the

Nichelle Nichols as Lieutenant Uhuru on Star Trek

Kennedy Space Center. Mae sought out Nichols there. When Nichols heard who was standing outside her dressing room door, she insisted that Mae be brought in immediately. Nichols gave Mae a warm hug, and the two have been friends ever since. In fact, Mae appeared on an episode of *Star Trek: The Next Generation*, which aired on June 6, 1992. The episode was called "Second Chances," and Mae played a character called Ensign Palmer.

THE LAUNCH OF THE *ENDEAVOUR*

Mae C. Jemison was thirty-six years old when she boarded the *Endeavour* on September 12, 1992. The *Endeavour* had been built to replace the *Challenger*, and this was the *Endeavour*'s second flight. The six other astronauts on the *Endeavour* were Robert L. "Hoot" Gibson, Curtis L. Brown, Mark C. Lee, Mamoru Mohri, Jerome "Jay" Apt, and N. Jan Davis. The *Endeavour* mission was important for many reasons and made quite a few firsts. In addition to Mae being the first African American woman astronaut, the *Endeavour* mission was the first time that a married couple— Lee and Davis—would go on a mission together. It was also the first time that a mission science specialist would be aboard a spacecraft, and it was the first joint mission between the United States and Japan.

Before the launch at the Kennedy Space Center at Cape Canaveral, Florida, Mae helped to get the space shuttle ready for the launch. She had

The crew of the STS-47 mission walks toward a bus wait-ing to take them to the launching pad on September 12, 1992. From there, they would blast into space for eight days, during which Mae helped to conduct experiments.

During her two years of training, Mae worked with a variety of people. Here, she trains with the mission specialist for space flight STS-29 and others. Together they inspect and discuss the mechanics of a test cell as part of their training.

to make sure that the thermal protection system was working properly. This system is composed of tiles on the outside of the shuttle that shield the spacecraft from heat when it reenters Earth's atmosphere. The reentry makes so much heat that without the thermal protection system, the spacecraft would burn up.

The flight was called the STS-47 Spacelab J. Mae knew that it was not only a fulfillment of her

Jerome Apt looks on as Mae trains to use the crew escape system. Each crew member practiced this technique as part of their training. The Johnson Space Center conducts many training exercises to help the astronauts get a feel for the equipment.

lifelong dream, but that her achievement was a symbol for many people. According to *Black Explorers*, Mae said, "It was the realization of many dreams of many people." In her interviews with the press, Mae made it very clear that, although she was the first African American woman astronaut, she was not the only African American astronaut at NASA. There were six others.

UP IN SPACE

Mae brought into space with her some items that had personal significance. She carried a poster of the Alvin Ailey dance troupe, from the dance production "Cry," which was specifically about African American women's struggles and achievements. She carried a flag from the Organization of African Unity, and a banner from the Mae C. Jemison Academy in Detroit, Michigan—an alternate public school established in 1992 to teach science and mathematics to children in preschool classes through the second grade. Some people criticized her choice of items to bring aboard, saying that she should have brought things that represented all people and not just African Americans. However, Mae Jemison had not had an easy road to get to be aboard the *Endeavour*, and it was important to her to bring objects that represented not only her struggle, but the struggle of her people, particularly African American women. She told Constance M. Green in an interview for *Ms.* magazine, "When I'm asked about the relevance to black people of what I do, I take that as an affront. It presupposes that black people have never been involved in exploring the heavens, but that is not so. Ancient African empires—Mali, Songhay, Egypt—had scientists, astronomers. The fact is that space and its resources belong to all of us, not to any one group."

Part of Mae's duties was to make the space shuttle into the laboratory they would need to conduct experiments. Mae was part of the blue shift, which was basically the night shift. The red shift was the day shift. Doctors Jan Davis and Jay Apt worked with Mae on the blue shift. The scientists conducted more than forty-four experiments, designed by scientists from across the United States and Japan. Some of these scientists worked for NASA and for NASDA, the Japanese Space Agency. Some of them were from universities or corporations.

They studied how the human body operates in weightlessness and how it responds to being in zero gravity. Mae designed an experiment to study

Mae and the other crew members do work in the Spacelab J module on September 12, 1992. This was Mae's second mission on the Endeavor, and it lasted eight days.

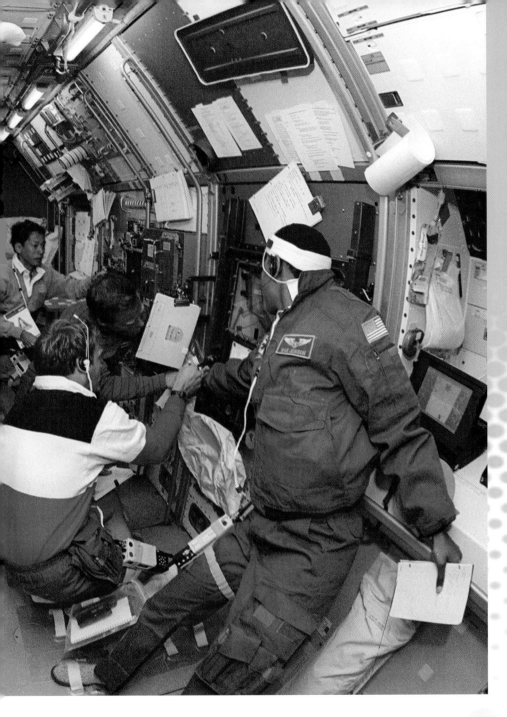

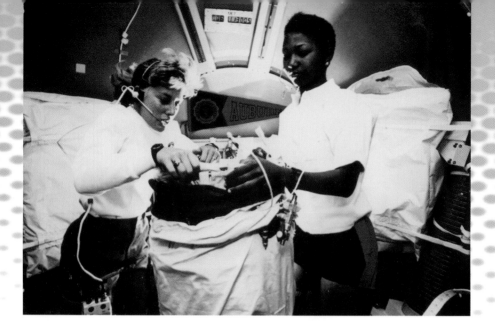

Mae and Jan Davis set up an experiment to test the way that air pressure affects the lower body. Many tests were done aboard the ship, including experiments on frogs' eggs to see if they would develop into tadpoles in such an unusual environment.

the effect of space travel on human bone cells. Astronauts can lose calcium from being in weightlessness a long time. The crew also did experiments with frogs' eggs to see whether fertilized frogs' eggs can develop into tadpoles in zero gravity. During the space flight, the astronauts talked by radio with schoolchildren all over the world. Mae talked with kids in her hometown of Chicago.

The *Endeavour* landed after eight days in orbit. The city of Chicago held a six-day celebration in honor of Mae Jemison, the first African American woman astronaut. The celebration took place on her thirty-sixth birthday on October 17, 1992. Mae had been an astronaut for six years, but only six months after her space shuttle flight, Mae resigned from NASA. According to *Black Explorers*, she said, "I leave with the honor of having been the first woman of color in space and with an appreciation of NASA—the organization that gave me the opportunity to make one of my dreams possible."

In her autobiography, she wrote, "Looking down and all around me, seeing the earth, the moon, and the stars, I felt just like I belonged right here, and in fact, any place in the entire universe." Mae Jemison had achieved her dream of going into space. What would she do once she had her feet on the ground again?

6

After NASA and Beyond

Mae Jemison, who had surprised the world by being the first African American woman astronaut, shocked the world when, six months after her space flight, she resigned from NASA. Mae wanted to get back to her goals of helping developing countries and teaching young people. But some people criticized her, saying that she had been hungry for fame and that she was not sincere about her desire to help people in developing countries through applying space technology.

In January 1993, Mae Jemison accepted a teaching position at Dartmouth College in New Hampshire. She taught a course about space-age technology in developing countries. She continued to teach at Dartmouth for six years. Mae also found time to devote her knowledge and experience to various organizations that bear her name.

THE JEMISON GROUP AND THE JEMISON INSTITUTE

When Mae left NASA in 1993, she founded the Jemison Group, Inc., a company that focuses on projects that combine social science issues with science and technology. Some of the projects on which the group has worked include Alafiya, which is a project that explores how to speed up and enhance health care in Africa by using a satellite-based telecommunication system. The group has also worked on designing solar-thermal electricity generating systems, which are ways of getting energy by harnessing the power of the sun. In addition to all of this great research, the group has introduced science and literature education into South Africa and has produced

3-D, real-time pilot-in-the-loop simulations for desktop computers, which help pilots learn how to fly aircraft.

Mae Jemison is also the director of the Jemison Institute for Advancing Technology in Developing Countries. It is an organization that researches, designs, and puts into real-life situations the newest scientific technologies.

THE DOROTHY JEMISON FOUNDATION FOR EXCELLENCE

Mae started the Dorothy Jemison Foundation for Excellence (DJF) to honor her mother, Dorothy Jemison. DJF is a not-for-profit organization. The organization runs on funds that various people and other organizations, including the government, give to DJF. DJF was organized to help schools and teachers make science more fun and challenging for the students. They do this by emphasizing more hands-on experiments, which are more fun than just sitting in a classroom listening to a teacher talk about science. DJF also encourages students to think about applying what they learn in science to benefit the world; that is, making a social contribution using scientific study.

The goals of the foundation are modeled after the teaching principals and life accomplishments of Dorothy Mae Jemison. Dorothy Jemison taught for more than twenty-five years in the Chicago public school system. Dorothy's personal formula for excellence can be seen not only in her teaching career, but in the success of her three children, who all went on to become successful members of society. Ada is a child psychiatrist, and Charles is a real estate broker. A major project of the Dorothy Jemison Foundation is The Earth We Share (TEWS).

THE EARTH WE SHARE

The Earth We Share (TEWS) is an international science camp, of which Mae is the director. The mission of the camp is to provide meaningful experiences in the sciences for teens. Mae herself

Mae lectured at Old Dominion University in Virginia on February 21, 2001. However, Mae did not spend all her time behind a podium. She took some time to talk to her audience, proving that Mae really takes an interest in others.

developed many of the programs and experiments conducted at the camp, and she works directly with the campers. Classes are held at colleges in the United States, such as Dartmouth College in New Hampshire and Talladega College in Alabama. Camp lasts for four weeks each summer. During that time, kids from all over the United States and countries around the world work with teachers and interns in teams

On March 26, 2002, Mae gave a lecture at Cornell University. Here, she talks with some of the audience members. Mae is known for her willingness to reach out to a younger set and inspire them to do great things. She is especially devoted to helping children.

of eight to ten students. The teams apply critical thinking skills to provide solutions to the problems that affect us globally. These problems could be anything from what to do about the greenhouse effect of industry, to how to solve the overpopulation problem. Some of the topics have included the following: Ways to determine if there is life elsewhere in the universe (and whether this life is intelligent life); predicting the hot public stocks of the year 2030; designing a crime control system for the year 2005; designing the world's perfect house; and designing an exercise program to keep high school students healthy. The teams create ideas about how to solve the problems. Then they create experiments in which they test their hypotheses. When the experiments are finished, kids evaluate the results of what they've done. In this way they can see how successful they've been at helping to solve world problems. Each topic requires the application of physics, mathematics, chemistry, biology, environmental sciences, and the social sciences.

BAYER CORPORATION AND THE MAKING SCIENCE MAKE SENSE PROGRAM

Since 1995, Mae has served as the national science literacy advocate for Bayer Corporation and its Making Science Make Sense program. Making Science Make Sense supports hands-on science learning in schools and helps ordinary citizens to

Bayer

Contact Us | Sitemap | Search | Help | Visit BayerUS |

| ome | About MSMS | Science Fun | Science Library | News | Our Communities |

n-Line Brochure
ational Spokesperson
verday Science
ayer Facts of Science
ducation Survey

ayer Links
ayer Global
ayer US

rms of Use
2000 Bayer Corporation

Meet Our National Spokesperson, Mae Jemison

Positive role models are an important part of a child's life. One way Bayer is bringing science education to life with children is through national spokesperson, Dr. Mae Jemison. In September 1992, Mae served aboard the space shuttle Endeavour as Science Mission Specialist. Here on Earth, she is a Bayer science advocate, talking with thousands of parents, students and teachers in Bayer site communities, helping them experience science in a hands-on, minds-on way.

■ Mae Jemison Biography

← Back to About Us

Home | About MSMS | Science Fun | Science Library | News | Our Communities

Mae is the national spokesperson for Bayer's Making Science Make Sense program, which aims to help young people learn about science. She reaches out to children, parents, and educators to stress the importance of science literacy.

understand how scientific studies can help benefit our planet and our quality of life.

Being an advocate means that Mae speaks in support of science literacy, or helping people have an easier time studying and reading about scientific subjects. Mae travels with Bayer executives around the country, encouraging teachers and school system officials to provide quality hands-on science education that stimulates students to think critically. Mae has visited about two dozen cities, meeting with thousands of people, including principals and school district administrators; federal, state, and local government officials; community leaders; and parents, teachers, and students.

RECOGNIZED FOR HER WORK

Throughout the years, Mae has been granted many honors. Some were given to her to recognize her hard work and contributions to society. Other awards were simply to acknowledge her selflessness and beauty, both inside and out.

Mae was selected as one of the nation's top seven women leaders in a poll conducted by the White House in January 1999; she was awarded the Kilby Science Award in 1993; she was inducted into the National Women's Hall of Fame in 1993; Johnson Publications gave her the Black Achievement Trailblazers Award in 1992; *McCall's* magazine named her one of 10 Outstanding Women for the '90s in 1991. Mae also holds numerous honorary doctoral degrees. She was even named one of *People* magazine's World's 50 Most Beautiful People in 1993, for her stunning good looks.

Mae was the subject of a PBS documentary, called *The New Explorers*. She also hosted and served as the technical consultant on *World of Wonder*, a weekly television program that aired on the Discovery Channel from 1994 to 1995. Mae serves on the board of directors of Scholastic, Inc., a children's book publishing company; the Aspen Institute, a nonprofit organization devoted to giving world leaders the tools to improve the quality of life; the Keystone Center, a nonprofit organization whose aim is to improve science education by introducing hands-on projects; the National Urban League, a nationwide organization that spreads information on civil rights and racial equality; and Spelman College, an all-women's, historically black college in Atlanta, Georgia.

Mae Jemison has been a dancer, an astronaut, a doctor, a scientist, and a teacher. Having

Bill Kurtis, host of the television show The New Explorers, *poses with Mae in March 1993. Bill, like Mae, used his celebrity status to promote awareness of various science-related issues. His television show brought science into the living rooms of people across America.*

achieved her dream of going into space, Mae Jemison has spent her time since her *Endeavour* mission trying to make planet Earth a better place for everyone on it. What does she have in mind as the next step of her fabulous career? In a February 2002 interview that ran in the *Virginian-Pilot*, the forty-five-year-old Mae said, "I'm still deciding what I want to be when I grow up next year."

TIMELINE

1956   Mae Jemison is born October 17, in Decatur, Alabama.

1972   Mae graduates from high school at the age of sixteen and heads to Stanford University in California.

1977   Mae receives a B.S. in chemical engineering and qualifies for a B.A. in African and Afro-American studies from Stanford University.

1981   Mae graduates from Cornell University medical school in New York City.

1982   Mae completes a one-year medical internship at the Los Angeles County/University of Southern California Medical Center.

1983   Mae spends two years working as a Peace Corps medical officer in Sierra Leone and Liberia, West Africa, overseeing the health care for all Peace Corps workers in those two areas. While there, she also does medical research, writes self-care manuals, and serves as a general practitioner.

1987	NASA accepts Mae into their astronaut program after a rigorous application and interview process.
1992	On September 12, the *Endeavour* is launched, with Mae as the mission specialist aboard the spacecraft. Mae becomes the first African American woman in space.
	Mae is awarded the Kilby Science Award. That same year, she is inducted into the National Women's Hall of Fame in Seneca Falls, New York.
1995	Mae begins working with the Bayer Corporation and its Making Science Make Sense program as the national science literacy advocate.
2001	Mae's autobiography, *Find Where the Wind Goes: Moments from My Life*, is published.

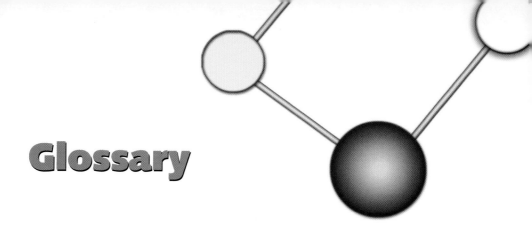

Glossary

antibodies Chemicals that the body makes to fight disease.

bionics A branch of science that seeks to enhance biological function with the help of electronics or mechanics.

cadaver A human corpse.

claustrophobia The fear of being in small, enclosed spaces.

diorama A small model of something.

dysentery A disease that is marked by dehydration due to severe diarrhea.

evolution How something changed over time or came into being.

grant A sum of money given to someone to help pay for his or her education or study.

hematology A science that deals with the blood.

hypothesis A guess at the outcome of a study.

integrated A term meaning that there is no separation of people of different races.

internship A period of work or study during which students learn more about a chosen career.

kibbutz A farming community in which all members of the community work and share equally.

malnutrition When the body is not getting enough of the vital nutrients it needs to maintain health.

militant Aggressive; engaged in combat.

obstetrics A branch of medicine having to do with childbirth.

pediatrics A branch of medicine having to do with children.

physiology The study of the human body's systems.

satellite A man-made object put into outer space to deliver information to scientists on the ground.

MAE JEMISON

supersonic Faster than the speed of light.

vaccine A substance that is given to people to protect them from a certain disease.

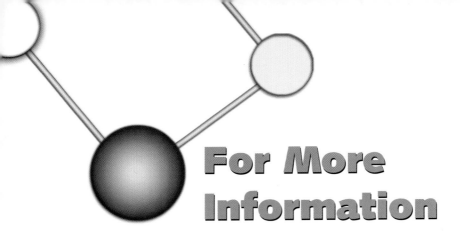

For More Information

The Earth We Share (TEWS)
The Dorothy Jemison Foundation for Excellence
P.O. Box 591455
Houston, TX 77259
(281) 486-7918
Web site: http://www.maejemison.com

NASA
Headquarters Information Center
300 E Street SW
Washington, DC 20546-0001
(202) 358-0000
Web site: http://www.nasa.gov

The National Women's Hall of Fame
76 Fall Street
P.O. Box 335
Seneca Falls, NY 13148
(315) 568-8060
Web site: http://www.greatwomen.org

Peace Corps

The Paul D. Coverdell Peace Corps Headquarters

1111 20th Street NW

Washington, DC 20526

(800) 424-8580

Web site: http://www.peacecorps.gov.

WEB SITES

Due to the changing nature of Internet links, the Rosen Publishing Group, Inc., has developed an online list of Web sites related to the subject of this book. This site is updated regularly. Please use this link to access the list:

http://www.rosenlinks.com/whfms/mjem/

For Further Reading

Black, Sonia W. *Mae Jemison*. New York: Mondo Publishing, 2000.

Burby, Liza N. *Mae Jemison*. New York: PowerKids Press, 1997.

Canizares, Susan. *The Voyage of Mae Jemison*. New York: Scholastic, Inc.., 1999.

Jackson, Garnet N. *Mae Jemison, Astronaut*. Columbus, OH: Modern Curriculum, 1994.

Jemison, Mae. *Find Where the Wind Goes: Moments from My Life*. New York: Scholastic, Inc., 2001.

Yannuzzi, Della A. *Mae Jemison: A Space Biography*. Springfield, NJ: Enslow Publishers, 1998.

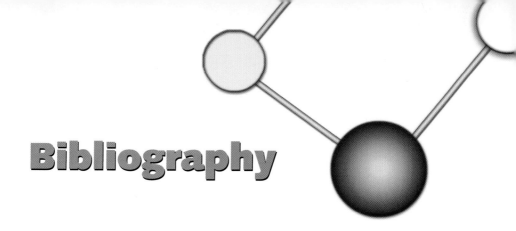

Bibliography

Bolden, Tonya. *And Not Afraid to Dare*. New York: Scholastic, Inc., 1998.

Dorsey, Kristen. "Ex-Astronaut Wants to Help Youths Launch Their Futures." *The Virginian-Pilot*, February 22, 2002.

Jemison, Mae. *Find Where the Wind Goes: Moments from My Life*. New York: Scholastic, Inc., 2001.

Phelps, J. Alfred. *They Had a Dream: The Story of African-American Astronauts*. Novato, CA: Presidio, 1994.

Reef, Catherine. *Black Explorers*. New York: Facts on File, 1996.

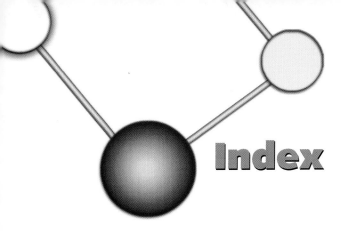

Index

Index

ABOUT THE AUTHOR

Magdalena Alagna is an editor and freelance writer living in New York City.

CREDITS

Cover and background image © PhotoDisc; cover inset and pp. 84–85, 86 © Marshall Space Flight Center; p. 12 © Steve Vidler/SuperStock; p. 16 © www. cuip.uchicago.edu; p. 18 © Sandy Felsenthal/ Corbis; p. 19 © Hulton-Deutsch Collection/Corbis; p. 21 © Underwood & Underwood/Corbis; pp. 23, 64, 73 © AP/Wide World Photos; p. 30 © Rod Searcy/AP/ Wide World Photos; p. 35 © Linda A. Cicero/Stanford News Service; pp. 39, 55, 77 © Bettmann/Corbis; p. 44 Courtesy of NewYork Weill Cornell Medical Center Archives; p. 48 © Wolfgang Kaehler/Corbis; p.57 © www.peacecorps.org; pp. 60, 63, 71, 80, 81 © Johnson Space Center/NASA; p. 74 © Timepix/NASA; p. 76 © Roger Ressmeyer/NASA/Corbis; p. 79 © NASA/Corbis; p. 92 photo by Dr. Linda Bailey Haydens; p. 93 © Frank DiMeo/Cornell University Photography; p. 95 © www.BayerUS.com; p. 98 © The Everett Collection.

DESIGN AND LAYOUT

Evelyn Horovicz

SERIES EDITOR

Eliza Berkowitz